M000081734

Jesus Came Out of the Tomb... So Can You!

A Brief Explanation of
Resurrection-based Christianity

by
Harold R. Eberle

Worldcast Publishing
Yakima, Washington,
USA

Jesus Came Out of the Tomb...So Can You!
A Brief Explanation of
Resurrection-based Christianity

Worldcast Publishing
P.O. Box 10653
Yakima, WA 98909-1653
(509) 248-5837
www.worldcastpublishing.com
office@worldcastpublishing.com

ISBN 978-1-882523-30-X
Cover by Paul Jones

Unless otherwise stated, all biblical quotations are taken from the *New American Standard Bible* © 1977, The Lockman Foundation, La Habra, California 90631.

Credits and Thanks

Pastor James Leuschen, of Spokane, WA, has been a constant catalyst in my journey to discover freedom and life in Christ. He can present many of the related truths in a more scholarly way than I can, therefore, to the more studious Christian I recommend his book entitled, *Good News for Mortal Man*.

I also want to thank others who furthered my understanding, including Pastor Ted Hansen, Pastor Svetoslav Petrov, and Rev. Keith Gerner. Other friends read through the original manuscripts, challenging me on several points and making me clarify my beliefs, including Andrew Bresmiester, John Alcamo, Pastor Cesar Dominguez, Todd Homer, and Peter Eisemann.

James Bryson is my most critical editor and after he destroys my initial attempts at writing, I always have to dedicate several more months to incorporate and recover from his criticisms. Annette Bradley, my final editor, is the expert with an eye for detail.

Thanks to all of you.

Table of Contents

Introduction

I was asked to speak in a church located in the heart of the Bible Belt of the United States. The senior pastor only knew me through one of my books, so he was taking a chance by allowing me into his pulpit. I was troubled immediately when I walked into his sanctuary and saw the pulpit raised high above the people. It felt oppressive. A huge cross hung at the front of the sanctuary. When the worship proceeded, all the songs centered around the death of Jesus and the need to surrender our lives to God. When the senior minister took the offering, he stood behind the elevated pulpit and spoke from the perspective of the cross of Jesus. He exhorted the people to die to themselves and give to God.

I was concerned deeply. Whenever I visit a church centered on the death of Jesus, rather than the life and person of Jesus, I want to shout good news, declare freedom for the people, and break their chains.

After the minister took the offering, he turned the pulpit over to me. I climbed the pulpit tower and greeted the congregation, but it didn't feel right, so I descended to ground level and talked to them on a more personal level. I noticed that the senior minister was uncomfortable with me leaving his high perch. He grew increasingly upset as I spoke to the people about the life available to us through Jesus Christ.

The next morning I learned how upset the pastor really was. He had decided to cancel the rest of my meetings. The veins in his neck bulged as he spoke of his passion for the cross of Jesus, and how he firmly believed that the cross must be the center of every church service. He complained about another church located nearby which emphasized joy, abundant life, and freedom. The leaders of that church were not leading their people to repent of their sins, and hence, he doubted whether the people in that church were truly saved.

Several times during our intense conversation the pastor defended his position, saying: "The apostle Paul declared, 'The *cross* is the power of God for salvation!'" It was not until an hour into the discussion that I was able to tell him that the phrase he had been quoting is not in the Bible. What the apostle Paul actually said was:

> *For I am not ashamed of the gospel, for it*
> *is the power of God for salvation....*
> (Rom. 1:16)

The Gospel—not the cross—is the power of God. The emphasis is on the good news. When I pointed this out the pastor was stunned.

I have seen such a reaction in many Christians' lives. They want to believe a certain way, so they actually memorize Bible verses, inserting words which they think should be there but really are not. Further distorting our individual understanding of

2

the Scripture is the fact that we all have heard passages taught from a certain perspective. Our individual perspectives may be wonderful, but they always are limited. Therefore, we must listen and consider how others understand the Scriptures to see if they are seeing things which we have not discovered.

After a long discussion, the pastor's anger subsided, and he agreed to let me speak at one more meeting, but he assigned me the topic and forbade me to pray over any of his people at the end of the service.

I am grateful to God for His manifesting presence. In the second meeting, God came and blessed the people in a deep and wonderful way. The pastor, who certainly loves God and is trying his best to please Him, recognized the presence of God and allowed me to minister at two more meetings with no restrictions.

I departed from that church in good relationship with the pastor, but I do not think he understands what is meant by Life-giving Christianity (also referred to as Resurrection-based Christianity). I hope he and thousands of other Christian leaders will consider the implications for their own lives and the lives of people to whom they minister.

Chapter 1
Sam Kneels beneath the Cross

Most Sunday mornings Sam arrives at church early to pray. His wife doesn't mind; she can get their two small children ready by herself, and besides, she wants to give Sam the space he needs to get himself right before God.

Ever since becoming a Christian three years ago, Sam has struggled to keep his mind on the things he knows he should be doing—taking care of his family, serving the church, being molded into a Christian man. But since the brief euphoria of his conversion, his life has descended into inner turmoil. He knows he must fight the good fight of faith; he has been taught that he must crucify himself daily in order to win the crown of glory; he is convinced that he must surrender his wicked heart completely, as Christ Himself surrendered all on the cross.

He thought he had done all that last Sunday. Pastor Gale delivered a moving message and Sam felt so convicted of his own sinfulness that he went forward and re-dedicated his life to God. He cried. He broke. He experienced God's forgiveness.

Yet, here he was, one week later, kneeling at the same altar. As he prayed, Sam recited phrases derived from Scripture: "There is no good thing in me, that is, in my flesh. The human heart is wicked and deceitful. I must decrease; You must increase. My life is nothing. You are everything. Not my will but Your will be done. I must die, that Christ may live in me."

5

Sam is not a sinner in the conventional sense. He doesn't get drunk, cheat on his wife, or steal when nobody's looking. He does lose his temper at times, and he gets frustrated with his children. His wife says he withdraws too much, and he knows that he should not let himself be depressed. But Sam isn't as concerned about these problems as much as he is about what he considers to be his chief failing. You see, Sam dreams. And he believes that his dreams will lead him into error and cloud his focus to become a man of God.

Sam dreams of owning his own business, but he fears that his motive is a desire for wealth and independence. So he stays at the job his father-in-law gave him a few months ago, managing home rentals. He hates it, but he believes that it's his flesh which is rebelling and that the process of subduing those desires will be good for him in the long run. Sam also dreams of going back to college, but with two small children for which to care, Sam also sees this as a selfish desire. Finally, Sam dreams of things that he will face only when he is too weak to resist them, such as running along a moonlit beach holding the hand of a beautiful woman whose face he sometimes can see, sometimes not. He cannot bring himself even to name the sins he believes are behind that vision, but it disgusts him thoroughly that as a Christian he even could imagine such evil.

That Sunday morning, Sam bowed his head against the carpet of the altar. When his aching heart could pray no longer, he looked into himself to see if his guilt and self-revulsion had left. After sensing its continued presence, Sam concluded with a desperate sense of failure that his surrender to the Lord was not in total, that deep in his treacherous heart he must be holding something back, keeping something from the Lord, something that his fleshly self finds too precious to give up, some sinful treasure that he cannot sacrifice to God, at least not for very long.

Sam got up from the carpet with no answers. Putting on his welcoming smile, he began greeting people as they arrived in the church lobby. It was wonderful seeing everyone, family, friends—real friends. He honestly loved the people. A few quick words put him back in touch with each one. He belonged. He even felt a certain respect and sense of responsibility here. He knew this was his church home.

When worship started, the people were more enthusiastic than usual, so it was quite uplifting, and Sam was able to bathe for a moment in the love of God. How grateful he was for all God had provided: family, job, health, and friends.

When Pastor Gale came to the pulpit, Sam was comfortably sitting with his arm around his wife. Life was good.

Pastor Gale always brought a truth from the Scriptures from which each person could find a few nuggets. Then Pastor drew the service to a close—as he always does—reminding people of their sinfulness, hinting about how evil this present world is, and quietly, yet firmly, telling the people of their need for Jesus and His sacrificial death. Pastor Gale then invited people who felt convicted of sin to come forward for prayer.

A handful of people responded. Sam knew he could go forward and kneel with them again. He knew better than anyone the carnality of his own thoughts. He easily could number himself among those at the altar.

But this Sunday Sam decided to stay seated. Not that he was rebelling or disagreeing with anything Pastor Gale had taught, but he had been there so many times before. He had tried to die to everything within. Would it do any good to go forward one more time?

In reality, Sam could not afford to go up there. He couldn't publicly walk to the front again, kneel in humility before God, and then walk away...only to battle with the same thoughts. Sam could not allow himself to accept the fact that he found no power for freedom at the altar. He knew without a doubt that Jesus is real, but he had embraced all that his church was offering, and he had not found any real freedom from the battles raging in his mind. If he went forward one more time and it did not help, Sam knew it would devastate his faith. It was too risky. It was safer to stay seated.

Chapter 2
Resurrection and Ascension Power

Sam may find forgiveness of sin at the cross and death of Jesus, but he only will find power over sin in the resurrection and ascension of Jesus. Unfortunately, no one has taught Sam this truth which is able to set him free.

Please allow me to explain.

When Jesus suffered on the cross, He took on the sins of the world. Then He died, for the wages of sin is death (Rom. 6:23).

After Jesus willing submitted to death, God the Father poured His Spirit, life, and glory into the Son. As Jesus rose from the dead, He overcame the power of death. When He ascended into heaven, all evil was positioned under His feet. He ascended to be Lord and King over all.

I cannot emphasize enough how great of an event this was.

When Jesus came out of the grave, the power of death was conquered. When Jesus ascended into heaven, the whole universe shifted. Every power that existed was placed under the authority of Jesus Christ.

God's mightiest work in history was not when He created the universe. It was not when He spoke the stars into existence. It was not when He said, "Let there be light." The greatest release of God's power was when He looked down at His dead Son and breathed into Him, raising Him to life and elevating

Him far above all rule and authority. That was the time in history when God flexed His muscles and demonstrated to the whole universe His glory and majesty.

The Greatest Release of God's Power

Resurrection & Ascension

That release of power accomplished something for our lives. This is what I want to explain to you. But first you must grasp the grandeur of our Lord's resurrection and ascension.

Think of a stick of dynamite. If you light the fuse it quickly burns away carrying the spark into the interior of the dynamite. Then the explosion occurs. The death of Jesus was similar to the fuse burning away. The resurrection and ascension of Jesus were the explosion and release of power.

10

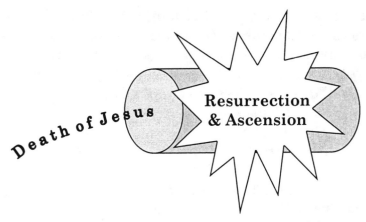

The power of Jesus' resurrection and ascension was greater than a stick of dynamite. It was greater than any nuclear explosion. It was more magnificent than a supernova. It was the greatest release of power in the whole universe.

Many Christians never will comprehend the greatness of this power, because their minds are fixated on the death of Jesus. One Bible verse that often is used to keep Christians focused on the death is I Corinthians 2:2, where Paul wrote:

> *For I am determined to know nothing among you except Jesus Christ, and Him crucified.*

With this verse firmly planted in their minds, some Christians are unable to move their eyes to the resurrection and ascension of Jesus.

In reality, such a fixation is based in a misunderstanding of Paul's words. Of course, Paul was unshakeable on the fact that Jesus was crucified. You and I must be firm on that truth also. But we must not lock that one phrase in our minds without considering other Bible verses with equal determination. For example, Paul wrote to the Philippians how he counts all things as loss in view of knowing:

> ...*Him* [Jesus Christ] *and the power of His resurrection....* (Phil. 3:10)

The main point is that we know Jesus Christ. It is the Jesus Christ Who died and rose again. While we get to know Him, we also should endeavor to know the power released in His resurrection and ascension.

Notice that Paul talked about the *power* of our Lord's resurrection. It is not merely the historical fact that Jesus rose again. Nor is it just the meaning of the resurrection. Paul endeavored to know the *power*.

That power which raised Jesus from the grave is available for us today. Please allow me to explain.

Chapter 3
The Power Directed toward Us

Paul prayed for the early Christians:

*I pray that the eyes of your heart may be
enlightened, so that you will know...what
is the surpassing greatness of His power
toward us who believe.* (Eph. 1:18-19a)

Paul went on to explain that the power directed
toward us is the same power which raised Jesus from
the dead and lifted Him into heaven.

*These are in accordance with the
working of the strength of His might
which He brought about in Christ, when
He raised Him from the dead and seated
Him at His right hand in heavenly
places.* (Eph. 1:19b-20)

Not only will we be resurrected from the grave at
some point in the future, but the power which
resurrected Jesus from the grave 2,000 years ago is
right now flowing toward Christians living on Earth.

Not only is resurrection power flowing toward us,
but also our Lord's ascension power. There is a literal
power available to us today. It is the same power
which elevated Jesus into heaven.

I pray that the eyes of your heart will be opened
to grasp this truth.

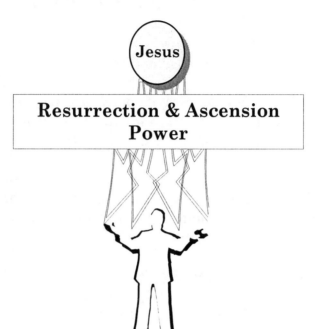

The power which flows from heaven is Life itself.
When Jesus arose, He became a Life-giving Spirit
(I Cor. 15:45). When He ascended, the Father gave
Him the Holy Spirit to pour out upon the world (Acts
2:33). Now Life and Power is flowing forth from Jesus
as He sits on His throne in heaven.

Those who believe in Jesus will have this Life
flowing from their innermost beings (John 7:37-38).
They will experience springs of living water flowing
in their hearts (John 4:14). That Life is able to free
people from the power of death and sin.

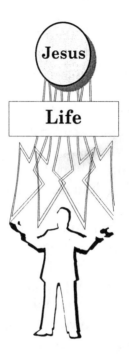

When Jesus sat down on His throne, He established a new government—a new Kingdom. All who enter into His Kingdom come under His authority and into His power. They are transferred from the domain of darkness and brought into the Kingdom of Light and Life. No longer does humanity have to live under the power of sin and death. Those who believe can enter into His freedom today.

It is interesting that Paul prayed for Christians to understand this truth. He prayed that "the eyes of your heart may be enlightened..." (Eph. 1:18). Indeed, it requires a work of God in the minds and hearts of people to grasp this truth. Just as it requires the grace of God for people to grasp the significance of our Lord's death, so also it takes His grace to come to the realization of the power available to us through His resurrection and ascension.

For many years as a Christian and as a pastor of a church, I wrestled with Paul's words, "to know Jesus Christ and the power of His resurrection..." (Phil. 3:10). I began praying that God would open the eyes of my heart. I meditated on the power of His resurrection. Even though I had been a Christian for many years, I did not feel as if I were fully experiencing the wells of life springing up within me which Jesus promised (John 4:14). For years I had believed and been teaching about the significance of our Lord's death. However, I never grasped the power released through His resurrection and ascension.

A glimpse of that power has changed my life. It is because of the resulting freedom which I have experienced that I am compelled to share it with others. I pray that the eyes of your heart will be opened. I also ask that you pray this prayer for yourself.

All Christians have heard how Jesus died for the forgiveness of their sins. Yet, millions do not understand why Jesus rose from the dead. To them, the death of Jesus is considered God's highest achievement for humanity. The resurrection and ascension of Jesus are seen primarily as afterworks in order to prove that Jesus was the Son of God and, therefore, His death was significant. They are so fixated on the death of Jesus that they have a difficult time understanding the power of His resurrection and ascension.

That is *Death-centered Christianity*. I want to contrast it with and teach you about *Life-giving Christianity* (also called *Resurrection-based Christianity*).

As I continue, please do not think that I am minimizing the significance of our Lord's death. Of course, His death was necessary for the forgiveness of our sins. Without His death, no human being can be reconciled to God. Only through the death of Jesus are we permitted a relationship with God the Father.

However, consider the words of Paul:

> *For if while we were enemies we were*
> *reconciled to God through the death of*

His Son, much more, having been reconciled, we shall be saved by His life.

(Rom. 5:10)

According to this verse, the *death* of Jesus accomplishes one thing for us and the *life* of Jesus accomplishes something entirely different. Do you see the distinction? The death of Jesus *reconciles us to God. His life saves us.*

You are not saved because Jesus died. At the cross forgiveness was established, but our salvation is gained through the resurrection life of Jesus Christ. Furthermore, the salvation about which Paul wrote in Roman 5 is not only salvation from hell. He was speaking of salvation from the power of sin and death in this world. He declared that we could "reign in life" through Jesus Christ (Rom. 5:17). Through the life of Jesus you can be delivered from the power of evil.

Remember Sam? He cried at the foot of the cross so many times that he began to question if there were any help available to free him from sin. He wanted to be godly but he never found the power. The church he attended wonderfully declared the work that Jesus accomplished at the cross, but they did not understand why Jesus rose and ascended into heaven. They offered forgiveness of sins, but not power over sin.

Sam only will find answers—true answers—when he orients his heart toward Jesus Who is in heaven. He must realize that Jesus is the Source of Life and Power. It is not His cross, but He Who sits on the throne pouring out love, grace, and victory on our behalf.

18

Through several years of sharing this truth with thousands of Christians, I have observed the reaction of many people. Some have discovered a path very similar to the one I am walking. Others have hopes rise in their hearts that they finally may discover freedom from sin and weaknesses with which they have struggled for years. Most have to hear this truth several times before they actually can grasp it. A few react negatively, concluding that I am challenging the very foundation of the Christian faith, which for them always has been the death of Jesus on the cross.

Those who react negatively may graciously give me the opportunity to expound upon the resurrection and ascension of Jesus, but they still cling tightly to the cross. When they hear me emphasize the resurrection and ascension, they try to make room in their minds to see the life of Jesus on equal terms with the death of Jesus. More than once I have had sincere Christians suggest that we need to see the death and resurrection of Jesus as two equal pillars supporting the truth of the Gospel.

If, indeed, we are talking about the reality of historical events, then the death and resurrection stand on equal footing. However, two pillars supporting the Gospel is an inadequate analogy to refer to the accomplishments of the death and resurrection. As I already explained, the death is as a dynamite fuse burning away, and the resurrection is the resulting explosion. Another good analogy is to see the death of Jesus as an entry point or a doorway into a huge building. Once a person has entered the building through the cross, they can live in the resurrection and ascension of Jesus. There they can abide in His infinite Life and Power.

In my endeavor to impact your mind and heart with the grandeur of our Lord's life, you may feel that I am minimizing His death. That is not my intent. I simply want to open you to what has been made available through the resurrection and ascension of Jesus.

Jesus is the Giver of life. He is life (John 11:25). He is the way, the truth, and life (John 14:6). "In Him was life, and the life was the light of men" (John 1:4). Jesus is the "bread of life" (John 6:35) which "gives life to the world" (John 6:33).

I want to be sure that you are identifying *Jesus* as the Source of Life. It is not His death on the cross which is the source. It is the Person Jesus Christ. It is He Who now sits at the right hand of the Father in heaven. Look to Him, not to the cross.

Chapter 5
Grace Flows from Jesus and His Life

From where does grace flow?

Death-centered Christianity looks to Jesus' death on the cross. Life-giving Christianity looks to Jesus Himself Who is alive in heaven.

The writer of Hebrews directs us to heaven where the throne of grace is located:

> *Therefore let us draw near to the throne*
> *of grace, so then we may receive mercy*
> *and find grace to help in time of need.*
>
> (Heb. 4:16)

According to this verse, we should look to God in heaven as the Source from whence grace flows.

Why do people in Death-centered Christianity look, instead, to the cross? Not only are they fixated upon the death of Jesus, but they tend to be confused about the definition of grace. Looking to the cross, they see forgiveness of sins and call that the work of grace. They typically define grace as "unmerited favor."

In reality, grace is much more than forgiveness. It is more than unmerited favor. Certainly grace is unmerited—we do not deserve it. However, to define it as "favor" does not say enough. Grace is more than God's kindness, or acceptance, or approval. In truth, *grace is God's life, power, nature, help, energy, and love all freely being poured out upon us.*

Christians immersed in Death-centered Christianity tend to confuse mercy and grace. Consider the following analogy to help distinguish these two gifts of God.

If you were driving your automobile too fast and a police officer caught you, you might plead with the officer not to give you a ticket. If the officer decides to let you go without giving any negative consequences, then you have received mercy, that is, you did not get what you deserved. On the other hand, if, for some unknown reason, the officer decides not only to let you go, but hands you $1,000,000 and says, "Have a nice day!", then you just received grace. Grace is when you *get* something which you do not deserve; mercy is when you *do not get* what you do deserve.

Seeing grace as more than mercy, we can identify *the avenue by which God administers grace.* Death-centered Christianity orients people to look to the cross as the avenue through which God's grace flows. In reality, God's mercy was established at the cross, but His mercy and grace flow from the Person of Jesus Christ Who rules from heaven.

Furthermore, Life-giving Christianity helps people see Jesus lavishing grace upon us. He freely is pouring out His life, power, help, and love. Grace includes everything of His nature freely being given to us. The proper response of believers is simply to receive God's blessings of mercy and grace.

Death-centered Christianity	Life-giving Christianity

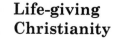

Too many Christians are being held at the cross of Jesus. The church they attend feels responsible to repeat the message of sin-and-death every service. The preacher wants to convince everyone they are sinners and then give them the answer, which is Jesus' death on the cross.

What if a church service were centered around Jesus Who overcame death? What if people were asked to respond to the King of kings and the Lord of lords? What if they came to the throne of grace and received life, power, help, and love? What would that release into the lives of believers?

Chapter 6
Repentance that Works

The term *repent* means "to turn, to change one's mind-set, or to orient one's life in another direction." How this turning applies to our lives depends upon whether you are listening to Death-centered Christianity or Life-giving Christianity.

Ministers trained in Death-centered Christianity want sinners to kneel at the foot of the cross, humble themselves, maybe cry out for forgiveness, and then turn away from the sins which they have committed. Of course, Christians with a Life–giving understanding of Christianity want people to stop sinning, but repentance entails something very different.

To see this, recall the message Jesus most often preached: "Repent, for the Kingdom of God is at hand!" With this declaration Jesus was announcing the arrival of a new Kingdom. He told people to turn their lives toward this Kingdom.

What is the Kingdom of God? After Jesus died, He resurrected, ascended, and sat down at the right hand of the Father. In His resurrection and ascension, Jesus conquered sin and death. He now is sitting on the throne of His kingdom.

To repent, for the Kingdom of God is at hand, is to escape the power of sin and death by entering into the Kingdom of God. Repentance, for the Christian with a Life-giving understanding, is to position oneself under a victorious Lord Who is pouring out His grace, that is, His life, power, help, and love.

	Death-centered Christianity	Life-giving Christianity
Repentance	Turn from Sin	Turn toward Jesus to receive His Life, Power, Help, and Love

John the Baptist preached repentance from sin, exhorting people to turn away from the sins they were committing (Luke 3:3). Of course, God wants us to stop sinning, however, there is a new message, a fuller Gospel. After John, Jesus Christ came to take away our sins in His death and overcome the power of sin in His resurrection and ascension.

A sinner who merely cries at the altar, asking God to forgive him, may find forgiveness of sins, but not necessarily freedom from sin.

When Sam cried at the altar, God forgave him, but Sam went out with the same problems with which he came. He still battled with thoughts which he could not control. He could not escape his self-loathing. Sam never stepped into a victorious life-style.

Power to overcome sins is obtained by yielding oneself to the Kingdom in which Jesus has conquered sin and death. That Kingdom consists of power (I Cor. 4:20). That Kingdom consists of righteousness, joy, and peace in the Holy Spirit (Rom. 14:17). As Jesus sits on His throne, He is pouring out the Spirit upon all flesh. Those who receive will have the Spirit flowing from their innermost beings as rivers of living water (John 7:38-39). That Spirit of Life overcomes sin and death in this world (Rom. 8:2).*

All those who put their faith in Jesus Christ enter into a new Kingdom. They also step into God's love under a New Covenant. Within this New Covenant people's sins are forgiven. In fact, there is no condemnation, for God does not even take into account their sins. Living in this New Covenant (of which I will teach more later) is to live under the constant bathing of God's love.

It is one thing to repent from sin, but it is another to repent toward the Kingdom of God. Please hear this! The reason Christians repeatedly find themselves going back to sinful ways is because they have not submerged themselves fully in the love of God. They still are holding themselves under shame and condemnation. They have not repented toward the Kingdom of God.

Some of my readers may insist on the need to include both repentance from sin and repentance toward the God of Kingdom. Indeed, both are important messages, but do not make the mistake of placing them on an equal level of importance. To repent toward the Kingdom of God is by far the key and most important message. This is the message Jesus preached.

---

* For a fuller explanation of what this means, I refer you to another book I have written entitled, *Grace, the Power to Reign.*

Chapter 7
Why Did Jesus Die?

Before I ask you to shift from Death-centered Christianity to Life-giving Christianity, it is only fair that I answer some pertinent questions. For the studious Christian, that includes some deeper theological questions, along with a basic understanding of how the Church historically became so immersed in Death-centered Christianity. If you are not interested in these more in-depth topics, feel free to skip the next eight chapters and jump ahead to chapter 15 where I return to explain how we can enjoy Life-giving Christianity. For those of you who first need to connect all of the dots in your mind, let's tackle the deeper questions.

Why did Jesus die on the cross?

According to Death-centered Christianity, God accomplished His greatest work in the death of Jesus. It was such a grand, all-inclusive work that everything else fades to insignificance. The death of Jesus on the cross is the pillar, focus, and center of Christianity.

Life-giving Christianity distinguishes between the works which God accomplished through Jesus'

1. death,
2. resurrection,
3. and ascension.

The Scriptures reveal that each was significant. Let's clarify the purpose for His death.

The death of Jesus was "the propitiation for our sins" (I John 2:2; 4:10; see also, Rom. 3:25; Heb. 2:17).* A propitiation is that which appeases another person or eliminates his or her anger.

For an example from ancient times of a propitiation, think of a king with his army determined to destroy a city. The leaders of that city may send a great gift to the king in hopes of appeasing him. If the king receives the gift and his anger subsides, then the gift has served as a propitiation.

For a modern example, envision a husband who has offended his wife. If she forgives him when he humbly offers a gift of flowers, then she has received his propitiation.

God sent His own Son to be the propitiation for our sins. His own Gift caused His anger to turn away from us, so that we could be reconciled to Him and receive His love.

Yet, Jesus did more than propitiate for us. On the cross He also *took on our sins*. This role was foreshadowed in the Old Testament times as the Jewish priest would place his hands on various sacrifice animals signifying how the sins of the people were placed on those animals (Lev. 4).

Our sins were placed upon Jesus.

As Jesus took on our sins, He had to die, because the wages of sin is death (Rom. 3:23). As He took on our sins, He submitted Himself to death.

In our Lord's death, another significant work was

---

* Some Bible translations use a word other than *propitiation*, but this word accurately conveys the meaning from the original Greek.

accomplished, for He established a New Covenant in which God will remember our sins no more:

> *"This is the covenant that I will make*
> *with them*
> *...their sins and the lawless deeds*
> *I will remember no more."* (Heb. 10:17)

God established this New Covenant, sealing it with the blood of His Son.

There are additional works accomplished in the suffering and death of Jesus but these prominently stand out and are most pertinent to our discussion. Jesus:

1. Propitiated for us,
2. Took on our sins,
3. Died for us,
4. Established a New Covenant.

Whether a person is convinced of Death-centered Christianity or Life-giving Christianity, they will agree that all four of these works were accomplished through the suffering and death of Jesus. However, there are other works about which they will disagree.

I already have explained how Death-centered Christianity sees the death of Jesus as the major avenue through which God's grace flows. A Christian embracing Life-giving Christianity will understand that the flow of God's mercy was established at the death of Jesus, while grace flows from the Person of Jesus Christ, Who now sits on His throne in heaven.

One other distinction which is important for our discussion is how Death-centered Christians will insist that *Jesus paid the penalty for our sins.* It is this point which I must challenge. According to Life-giving Christianity, this statement is not biblically accurate. This point is so important that I will take the next two chapters to clarify this distinction between Death-centered Christianity and Life-giving Christianity.

	Death-centered Christianity	Life-giving Christianity
Works accomplished through the death of Jesus	1. Propitiation for us 2. Took on our sins 3. Died for us 4. Established a New Covenant 5. Established the flow of God's grace 6. Paid the penalty for our sins	1. Propitiation for us 2. Took on our sins 3. Died for us 4. Established a New Covenant 5. Established the flow of God's mercy

Chapter 8
A Penalty for Our Sins?

Did Jesus pay the penalty for our sins?

To answer this, we first must define what a penalty is. Typically, we understand it to be a punishment imposed by someone of higher authority.

For example, in the United States the Internal Revenue Service has the authority to collect taxes. If the Internal Revenue Service catches someone who has neglected to pay his or her taxes, they will enforce the law, making sure the person pays those taxes, but they also may impose a penalty, which typically consists of additional fines. That penalty is an *added punishment.*

When we speak of the penalty for sin, we are not referring to the consequences of sin. Sin has many consequences as the effects of sin work in a person's life. Those consequences include shame, depression, discouragement, hopelessness, sickness, broken relationships, confusion, and a multitude of other negative results. Those are the natural outworkings of sin, for the wages of sin is death (Rom. 3:23). These are in contrast to the penalty for sin, which is a punishment imposed by a just God.

When we ask if Jesus paid the penalty for our sins, we are asking if God the Father added to the pain which Jesus suffered? We already explained how Jesus took on Himself the sins of the world, and He suffered the consequence of sin, which is death. Did God the Father also take the penalty due us and place it upon Jesus? While Jesus was bearing the weight of all of our sins did the Father add to His suffering? Did He impose a penalty?

There is no verse in the Bible that states or implies that any penalty was applied or paid.

What the Bible teaches is that God *forgives* the sins of those who place their faith in Jesus. To forgive sin means that no penalty will be incurred. Or in other words, the *debt* has been forgiven. A debt that has been forgiven does not have to be paid by *anyone*.

This issue is important because it lies at the very foundation of the controversy between Death-centered versus Life-giving Christianity. It is so foundational we need to clarify it further.

We already saw how Jesus was a propitiation for our sins. A propitiation is not the payment of a penalty. Instead, it is a gift or action which wins the favor of another person *so a penalty will not have to be paid*.

To understand this more clearly, consider how Moses interceded for the Hebrew people. When God became angry and almost destroyed the Hebrews, Moses interceded and God changed His mind about doing harm to His people (Ex. 32:9-14). God did not demand that someone pay for the sins of the people. God did not take out His anger on Moses. Moses did not pay for the sins of the people. Because of his relationship with God, Moses interceded and God listened.

In a similar fashion, Jesus propitiated for us. He did not pay the penalty for our sins. There was no penalty, because God changed His mind, subdued His own anger, and forgave those who put their faith in Jesus.

Hearing this concept for the first time can be disturbing to many Christians because they have been told for so many years that Jesus paid the penalty for our sins. In reality, that concept is foreign to the Bible. It portrays a God Who is angry at humanity and Who took that anger out on Jesus. In truth, Jesus willingly interceded for us, asking the Father to forgive people of their sins. This plan was established between the Father and Son before the foundations of the world.

To better understand this perspective, we must understand how God deals with people through covenants. He is a covenant-making and covenant-keeping God.

In the Old Testament times, when lambs were offered by the priests in the Temple, the lamb's death did not pay for the sins of the people, but the blood reaffirmed the covenant of God with His people. Hence, God overlooked their sins.

Before Moses led the Hebrew people out of Egypt, each family killed a Passover Lamb whose blood was spread on the doorposts of their homes. The blood of the lamb did not pay for the people's sins, but it marked their home as a home under the protection of God so that the death angel would not visit that home.

As the Passover Lamb, Jesus was offered to establish God's covenant.

The writer of Hebrews tells us that without the shedding of blood there is no forgiveness of sins (Heb.

9:22). The Christian immersed in Death-centered Christianity interprets this to mean that blood pays the penalty for people's sins. However, the context explains that the blood of Jesus was "the blood of the covenant" (Heb. 9:20). When we read this in context, we realize that our Lord's blood was not to pay for sins, but to establish a covenant in which our sins will be remembered no more (Heb. 8:7-9:22).

The death of Jesus established a covenant; it did not pay a penalty. God forgave sins, hence, no penalty was imposed.*

---

* For more biblical terminology concerning what the blood and death of Jesus actually accomplished, consult the Appendix.

Chapter 9
Our Concept of God

Most Christians embrace a mixture of Death-centered Christianity and Life-giving Christianity. One moment they will declare that Jesus paid the penalty for their sins and the next moment they will talk about the covenant in which their sins are forgiven. They incorporate implications from one idea and the other. They try to hold contradictory beliefs at the same time, and, for the most part, they can get away with it because no one has challenged them to think through the issues.

If you honestly think about it, you will have to choose one or the other, and the consequences are far reaching.

Lying at the foundation of Death-centered Christianity is a concept of a God Who is angry at sin. He also is just in the sense that He must punish sin. God had to take out His anger on someone, so in His love He sent His Son to stand in for us. Jesus took on our just penalty.

In contrast, Life-giving Christianity recognizes a God Who is just, but He does not have to punish sin. Because He is sovereign, He can and does forgive sin. He does not have to demand the payment of a penalty. He is a forgiving God.

Furthermore, God is a covenant-making God. He deals differently with people who are in covenant with Him than He does with those outside of a covenant relationship. To see this difference, we can point

out that the wrath of God continues to abide upon
those who do not put their faith in Jesus (John 3:36).
A judgment day is coming when they will pay for
their sins. However, those who put their faith in Jesus are forgiven. God subdued His wrath. God truly
has forgiven those within covenant with Him.

	Death-centered Christianity	Life-giving Christianity
God's Nature	1. God is angry at sin 2. God is just in the sense that He must punish sin	1. God is forgiving 2. God is just, but He does not have to punish sin 3. God is sovereign in the sense that He can forgive sin 4. God is a covenant-making God who deals differently with those in covenant-relationship with Him

This understanding of God's nature is the most
fundamental difference between Death-centered
Christianity and Life-giving Christianity. Of course,
Death-centered Christianity will say that God is a
covenant-making God, but it is not seen as a central
characteristic of His nature. Life-giving Christianity
boldly declares that God is a covenant-maker, and,

therefore, He has no wrath and no condemnation toward those who are in covenant relationship with Him.

If, indeed, God forgives those who enter into covenant relationship with Him, then we will understand the death of Jesus to be the establishing and sealing of that covenant. Furthermore, the Father exercised *no anger* and imposed *no penalty* toward the Son.

On the other hand, if God is angry and just in the sense that He must punish sin (as Death-centered Christianity maintains), then Jesus became the object of His anger. He suffered the wrath of God.

Does the Bible teach that Jesus took on the brunt of God's anger? There is no Bible verse that says this, but Death-centered Christianity maintains that God's anger was the primary force behind the suffering of our Lord. He was stepping in the way as God released the fullness of His wrath toward sin. Jesus was tortured at the hands of the Father. Jesus was the shock absorber, so to speak, of the wrath of God.

Life-giving Christianity strongly objects to this view. If, indeed, Jesus took on the wrath of God for our sins, then there would be no more wrath to come in the future. If, indeed, Jesus was the shock absorber Who received the shock of God's wrath for the sins of the world, then there would be no more wrath to be released at a coming day of judgment. Yet, the Bible is clear that wrath is being stored up for a judgment day (Rom. 2:5; 5:9; Eph. 5:6; I Thes. 2:16). Seeing that wrath will be poured out in the future, we must conclude that Jesus *did not* take on the wrath of the Father when He was hanging on the cross.

Finally, consider this: What ultimately killed Jesus?

If God is just in the sense that He must punish sin, then we will understand the suffering and death of Jesus to be the payment for humanity's sin, as God took out His wrath on Jesus. Therefore, what ultimately killed Jesus was the wrath of the Father as Jesus paid our penalty.

In contrast, Life-giving Christianity sees the suffering and death of Jesus very differently. Jesus took on our sins and our sins killed Him, for the wages of sin is death.

	Death-centered Christianity	Life-giving Christianity
What killed Jesus?	The just wrath of God	The sins of humanity

Chapter 10
It Is about Relationship

If God is angry and just in the sense that He must punish sin, then people should hide behind the cross. If God focused all of His anger at the cross and that cross is the barrier between us and God's wrath, then we had better use the cross as a shield and leave nothing exposed.

In contrast, if a New Covenant was established for us at the death of Jesus, then we need not hide behind the cross. We can come out from behind it. In fact, as covenant people we can stand boldly in the presence of God Who forgives and loves us.

Not only does this change our concept of God; it changes our relationship to Him.

With the Life-giving concept of God, sin is no longer the biggest issue. Those who place their faith in Jesus enter into a covenant relationship with God. They become children of God. That relationship is the focal point of Life-giving Christianity.

Death-centered Christianity is never able to fully get out from under the cross and death of Jesus. Even though Christians are told that they are children of God, they consciously and subconsciously keep hidden behind the shield of Jesus and His blood. This dynamic between people and God is inescapable in Death-centered Christianity. It permeates every thought and every action of the Christian immersed in this way of thinking. It establishes a relationship between God and the Christian wherein forgiveness of sins is found, but that Christian remains ever conscious of those sins and hidden behind Jesus.

Death-centered Christianity revolves around two fixed points: the sinfulness of humanity and the death of Jesus. We can identify these as humanity's problem and God's solution.

In contrast, Life-giving Christianity sees that sin has been removed through a covenant. Therefore, sin is no longer the most important issue. Humanity's real problem is a broken relationship with God. The answer is a restored relationship through the covenant established through Jesus.

	Death-centered Christianity	Life-giving Christianity
Man's problem	Sin	Broken relationship
God's solution	Death of Jesus	Covenant relationship

The covenant relationship is one in which God is our Father and we are His children. As our Father, He is more concerned about us than He is about sin.

To see this, consider the parable Jesus told of the father with a prodigal son (Luke 15:11-32). The son squandered his inheritance and lived according to his sinful passions. When he returned to his father, his father ran out to greet him. The father did not demand a penalty to be paid for sins. The father's first and foremost concern was to receive his son back into relationship and restore his son. He threw his cloak over his son and put a ring on his finger. Of course, the father wished his son had not lived sinfully, but upon his son's return the father's main concern was for the welfare of his boy.

If you have a child who goes astray, what is your main concern? Is it anger that he or she is sinning or is it for the welfare of your child? If you love your child, then you want your child safe, secure, happy, and at home with you.

If we build on the concept that God is a loving Father Who has forgiven our sins, then we will develop Life-giving Christianity. In contrast, if we see God as an angry God Who must punish all sin, then we will be held within Death-centered Christianity.

I have good news to declare to those who have put their faith in Jesus: God is not angry with you. Jesus was the propitiation for us. There is *no* condemnation because God has forgiven you. God's heart toward you is love. He wants you in a close personal relationship with Him.

Chapter 11
The Historical Hold
Of Death-centered Christianity

Before we proceed to further develop Life-giving Christianity, it will be helpful to see how deep-seated Death-centered Christianity is within the Western world. Allow me to explain why much of the Church today is overly-focused on humanity's sin and the death of Jesus. Let's examine how this perspective developed in Church history.

In the early Church, Christian preaching primarily was focused on the life of Jesus. For example, when Peter preached on Pentecost Day, he mentioned the crucifixion (Acts 2:23), but he did not explain why Jesus died on the cross. Peter preached that Jesus worked miracles (vs. 22), rose from the dead (vs. 24-32), was exalted to the right hand of the Father (vs. 33-36), is the fulfillment of Old Testament prophecies, and received and poured forth the Holy Spirit (vs. 33). To this message, 3,000 people responded and were saved. Peter preached a similar message to Cornelius, without explaining the purpose of our Lord's death (Acts 10:36-43).

In the book of Acts we also have record of two full messages which Paul preached to unbelievers (Acts 13:16-41; 17:22-31). Neither message explains the death of Jesus, but both emphasize His resurrection.

It was not until the Fourth Century that the emphasis in teaching began to shift to the death of Jesus. As Christianity gradually was coming under the dominating influence of leaders in Rome, the Church began standardizing the liturgy of each service. Over the course of many years, the Roman Catholic Church developed *the Mass,* in which each church service was thought of as a reenactment of the death of Jesus. Crucifixes were positioned at the front of each church sanctuary. Priests stood before an altar and prepared communion for the people. The communion service, which is the very heart of the Roman Catholic Mass, was (and still is) seen by Roman Catholics as the *sacrifice of the Mass,* that is, the Lord sacrificing His life again for the people.

It was not until the Eleventh Century that a theologian named Anselm (c. 1033-1109) developed and communicated the idea that God took out His anger on Jesus on the cross.

This teaching became predominant in the Roman Catholic Church from the Twelfth Century forward and eventually found its way into Protestant thought.

Martin Luther and other leaders of the Protestant Reformation accomplished great things for Christianity, but they retained the Church's fundamental theological focus on the work accomplished through the death of Jesus. In fact, they increased the focus on His death. It was at this very point (in addition to Scripture being their final authority) that the Reformers most wanted to distinguish themselves from Roman Catholics. They saw in the death of Jesus that God's work was so complete that humans need add no good works to it. Simple faith in Jesus Christ made salvation available.

I cannot emphasize this point enough. The Protestant Reformation gave us a clearer understanding of the totality of what Jesus accomplished on the cross—we should be grateful for that. However, the leaders of the Reformation continued to focus Christianity on the sinfulness of humanity and death of Jesus, rather than on the life of Jesus.

Leaders such as John Calvin (1509-1564) further developed the thoughts of the Reformation. Calvinism became especially dominant in the churches of Scotland, Switzerland, and The Netherlands. This system of thought developed and became known as *Reformed Theology*. Holding especially tight to the views of Reformed Theology were the Huguenots of France and the Puritans of England. Those committed Protestant groups endured much persecution during the 1600s and 1700s, eventually spreading across Europe and then into North America.

When the Great Awakening hit North America, a leader named Jonathan Edwards (1703-1758) stepped out as the most bold, outspoken proponent of Reformed Theology. We can highlight his theology by mentioning the message for which he became most famous: "Sinners in the Hands of an Angry God." On several occasions when Edwards delivered this message listeners were so moved that they cried out in terror of God and His coming wrath. Upon this system of thought much of Protestant Christianity in both America and across Europe was founded.

Out of Reformed Theology has grown Evangelical Christianity, which today includes hundreds of denominations and Christian groups. Generally speaking, Evangelicals adhere to Death-centered theology, however most are not as rigid in their beliefs as

Reformed Christians. Among Evangelical Christianity, Reformed thinkers are as a big brother prominently sitting in every room where theology is being discussed.

Today the Christian groups which cling most tightly to Reformed Theology are the Christian Reformed Denomination, Presbyterian Churches, and most Baptist Denominations. Lutheran Theology also is Death-centered, but it is distinct from Reformed Theology. In the United States the region which has deepest roots in Protestant Christianity is known as the *Bible Belt,* and there theology focused on the death of Jesus is most deeply entrenched. Also, much of the preaching and teaching which comes across American Christian radio is profoundly influenced by Reformed Theology.

The theologies of Pentecostal and Holiness denominations typically are not considered Reformed, but you can be sure that Death-centered thinking is at the foundation of their theology if the minister repeatedly reminds people of their sinfulness and encourages them to come to the front of the church to repent from their sins.

What is important for our discussion to follow is how Death-centered Christianity (Reformed Theology being the most strict) revolves around two fixed points: *humanity's sin* and the *death of Jesus.* Or we can identify those points as: *humanity's problem* and *God's solution.* Of course, these are significant points that need to be addressed by followers of Jesus Christ; however, an over-emphasis on these two points has locked Christians in the Western world into a Death-centered form of Christianity.

Chapter 12
The Over-emphasis of Sin

Leaders anchored in Death-centered Christianity (or Reformed Theology) try hard to drive home these two points—the seriousness of people's sin and the grandeur of Jesus' death. Of course, all human beings sin and Jesus' death is awesome. However, building our theology around these two fixed points leads to a distortion of Christianity.

This distortion will become more and more obvious as we continue, but here I want to show you how Reformed Christians over-emphasize the sinfulness of humanity.

One Scripture often repeated by Reformed preachers is Isaiah 64:6, which says:

> *All of us have become like one who is*
> *unclean,*
> *And all our righteous deeds are like a*
> *filthy garment....*

Christians immersed in Reformed thinking like to use this verse to teach that everything a non-Christian does—even righteous deeds done to try to please God—are evil and detestable in God's eyes.

To see how wrong this interpretation is, all we have to do is read the context of Isaiah 64:6. The preceding verse tells us how God responds readily and willingly to people who do righteous deeds.

> *You meet him who rejoices in doing*
> *righteousness....*   (Is. 64:5)

God does not reject everyone's righteous deeds, but actually responds to and rewards people for the good they do. This is a principle repeated throughout the Bible, for God will reward every person according to his or her deeds. The writer of Hebrews tells us that God is a rewarder of all who seek Him (Heb. 11:6). In that same chapter the writer gives us many examples of people who lived in Old Testament times who sought God and obtained His favor.

Recognizing this, we must not conclude that every non-Christian's acts of righteousness are filthy garments in God's eyes. Contrary to what Reformed preachers would have us believe, Isaiah 64:6 neither is condemning nor rejecting acts of righteousness.

Read Isaiah 64:6 again.

> *All of us have become like one who is*
> *unclean,*
> *And all our righteous deeds are like a*
> *filthy garment....*

Notice how verse six says that they all *"have become like one who is unclean."** They were not always rejected by God. This verse actually is speaking of the Jewish people at a time when their rebellion against God had become so severe that God turned His favor away from them. In this passage, the prophet Isaiah

---

* This verb tense is not evident in some Bible translations but it is true to the original Hebrew Scriptures.

is crying out to God and recalling how God previously looked with favor upon them as a people, but then stopped being pleased with their righteous acts. Isaiah is speaking about the Jewish people during the time they were in exile being punished for their rebellion.

To remove verse six from its context and apply it to all people in every generation is a serious mistake. It is wrong to use that verse to teach that all the righteous deeds of non-Christians are detestable in God's eyes.

Reformed thinkers interpret other Bible verses through such a negative lens, as well. For example, the apostle Paul wrote:

> *For I know that nothing good dwells in me, that is, in my flesh....* (Rom. 7:18)

Some Christians take these words of Paul and from them mistakenly teach that nothing good dwells in us at all.

To see that this is the wrong interpretation, read the context of Paul's words. Throughout Romans chapter seven, Paul is explaining the conflict that happens within him because both good and evil are at war. Several times in that chapter, Paul mentions his desires to do good (i.e., Rom. 7:15, 21, 22). Seeing how many times he refers to the good element within his own being, we have to conclude that his words, "nothing good dwells in me, that is in my flesh," do not refer to his entire being. There also must be a good part in Paul.

Flesh refers to the carnal, corrupted part of our nature. Therefore, by definition, there is nothing good in our flesh. However, it would be wrong to say that our entire being is fleshly. That would contradict what Paul was saying about the conflict of good and evil within. There is no conflict if there is no good. Both good and evil exist within a person. Flesh is the evil portion.

Reformed Theology teaches that everything within the non-Christian is unprofitable. In fact, they teach that all humanity is "totally depraved," meaning totally and completely evil, unable even to ask God for help apart from God initiating and causing it within a person.*

Please let me show you a more biblically accurate view of humanity.

---

* Two other passages often used by Reformed thinkers to promote a very negative view of humanity are Romans 3:10-18 and Psalm 51:5-6. For a more positive understanding of these passage, I refer you to another book I have written entitled, *Precious in His Sight.*

Chapter 13
There Are Good People and Bad People

According to Reformed Theology, every non-Christian is totally evil to the core. Yet, the Bible gives us a very different view of humanity.

Throughout the Scriptures there are consistent contrasts between the good person and the evil person. Before there even were any Christians, the writer of Proverbs contrasted the good and the wicked (i.e., 12:2), the righteous and the unrighteous (i.e., 24:16), the wise and the foolish (i.e., 13:16).

As I discuss this, do not misinterpret what I am teaching. I am not implying that anyone can be saved apart from Jesus Christ. Whether a person is good or bad, they still need to believe in Jesus in order to be saved. Even good people sin from time to time. Every human being needs the forgiveness available only through Jesus Christ.

What I am doing here is challenging Death-centered Christianity which is strongly tied to the belief that all people are evil to the core.

Consider how Jesus viewed people when He said that God "causes His sun to rise on the evil and the good..." (Matt. 5:45). In this context, Jesus was not speaking about Christians being good. He was speaking about everyday people. According to Jesus, some people are good.

Consider also what Jesus said in the following passage:

> *"The good man brings good things out of*
> *the good stored up in him, and the evil*
> *man brings evil things out of the evil*
> *stored up in him."* (Matt. 12:35)

Jesus would not have said this if good people did not exist.

Of course, no human being is "good" in the sense of being perfect as God is perfect. We see Jesus differentiating between the goodness of people and the goodness of God when someone called Him "good teacher."

> *"Why do you call me good?" Jesus*
> *answered. "No one is good—except God*
> *alone."* (Mark 10:18)

Here, Jesus is making a statement about the goodness of humanity compared with the goodness of God. In that comparison, the goodness of God is perfection, something that no human being can attain. However, in a less strict sense, we can say that certain people are good.

In fact, many people in the Bible are referred to as good.

> *Now there was a man named Joseph, a*
> *member of the Council, a good and*
> *upright man....* (Luke 23:50-51)

Note that Joseph was not a Christian. He was a Jew, and yet the Bible refers to him as "good."

54

Job is said to be "blameless, upright, fearing God and turning away from evil" (Job 1:1).

A gentile named Cornelius and his family are referred to in this way:

> *He and all his family were devout and*
> *God-fearing....* (Acts 10:2)

Here is a family—not yet saved—called "devout and God-fearing."

Since the Bible tells us some people are good, it is wrong to say (as Reformed Theology says) that every person (before they become Christian) is totally depraved.

Again let me say that we all need Jesus and the forgiveness available to us through the New Covenant. However, not all people are evil.

Chapter 14
Life Is the Answer to Death

We have seen how Death-centered Christianity (which in its most rigid form is Reformed Theology) revolves around two fixed points: the sinfulness of humanity and the death of Jesus. Reformed preachers see these as humanity's problem and God's solution.

Life-giving Christainity says God's primary concern is not sin, but people and their relationships with Him. Because of a violated relationship, people need to be reconciled to the Father through Jesus Christ.

	Death-centered Christianity	Life-giving Christianity
Man's problem	Sin of humanity	Broken relationship
God's solution	Death of Jesus	Restored relationship

Further turning our focus away from sin, Life-giving Christianity goes on to say that humanity's secondary problem is the *consequence of sin*, which is encapsulated in the term *death*.

This *death* is not limited to the fact that we all will cease living one day. The *death* of which the Bible speaks includes all the consequences of sin, for the wages of all sin is death (Rom. 6:23). Death stems from a violated relationship with God, and it results in the corrupting influence of sin upon humanity, including discouragement, condemnation, weakness, hopelessness, sickness, depression, confusion, shame, lack of meaning and direction, etc.

Consider again the parable Jesus told of the father with a prodigal son. The father's first and foremost concern was not that his son had been sinning, but it was for the welfare of his son. Similarly, God the Father's foremost concern is for our welfare. He does not want us to suffer the consequences of sin. He does not want us to be estranged from Him. He does not want us lost in a sea of death. He does not want us to die.

If we truly think of God as a Father, eagerly receiving back His prodigal children, then it shifts the focus of our Christianity. Of course, the Father does not want His children sinning, but that is not His primary concern. He loves us and He does not want us to suffer the consequences of sin.

If *sin* is looked upon as humanity's primary problem (as Reformed Theology teaches), then the *cross and death of Jesus* always will be looked upon as the answer.

If we truly recognize God as Father, then we will see our relationship with Him as the thing which is of greatest concern to Him. Secondarily, we will understand that He is concerned for our welfare. He does not want us to die.

The answer to death is life. This life is available through Jesus Christ. Jesus came into the world not only to deal with sin, but also to give us life.

"...I came that they may have life, and

have it abundantly."   (John 10:10)

Jesus is speaking not only of the eternal life which will enable us to live forever; He also is speaking of His life which overcomes death in this world.

Jesus promised us, *"a well of water springing up to eternal life"* (John 4:14). Now we are partakers of divine life (II Peter 1:4). Jesus said:

> *"He who believes in Me, as the Scripture said, 'From his innermost being will flow riviers of living water.'"*   (John 7:38)

God's life is flowing in us right now.

	Death-centered Christianity	Life-giving Christianity
Man's Problem	Sin of Humanity	Death of Humanity
God's Answer	Death of Jesus	Life of Jesus

This marks a fundamental difference between Death-centered Christianity and Life-giving Christianity. In a church where the minister has been trained in Death-centered Christianity, the orientation of every church service will be on the sinfulness of humanity and the death of Jesus. In a church which is Life-giving, the minister will focus on our relationship with God and the new life available to us in Jesus.

Chapter 15
Meeting Jesus for Salvation

Every minister immersed in Death-centered Christianity wants to lead sinners to the cross of Jesus. With the help of the Holy Spirit, they will attempt to convince people that they are sinners and then offer the answer, which is Jesus' suffering and death.

Life-giving ministers have a different approach. One church I visited in Africa is known for the great number of people becoming Christians every week. The senior minister talks mostly about the miracles of Jesus and the love of God. At the end of almost every Sunday service the minister has a call forward. He stands at the front and says something such as this: "If anyone wants a relationship with God, come forward and meet Him now." It is very common for several hundred people to answer that call every Sunday morning.

From the perspective of Death-centered Christianity, it is doubtful that those people who answer that type of call forward truly are saved. They were not first convicted of their sins. They did not have the cross of Jesus explained in a way in which they would want to cry at the altar. They did not go through their formula of realizing humanity's problem and then applying God's solution.

Are they really saved? To answer this we must answer the question, "What is necessary for salvation?"

The apostle Paul answered this when he wrote:

...if you confess with your mouth Jesus as Lord, and believe in your heart that God raised Him from the dead, you will be saved. (Rom. 10:9)

Does a person have to understand why Jesus died on the cross in order to be saved? According to Paul's words in this passage the most important fact to know is that Jesus was resurrected from the dead. Salvation comes *not* when a person accepts the death of Jesus, but when they *believe* in the resurrection of Jesus and *confess* Him as Lord.

Consider the salvation of Cornelius, as recorded in Acts 10. In presenting the Gospel, Peter mentioned that Jesus died on a cross, but he did not explain why Jesus died. Instead, Peter focused on the life of Jesus: that He was anointed by God, healed the sick and demon oppressed (10:38), rose from the dead, and appeared to many witnesses (10:40-41). Peter ended his presentation saying:

"...everyone who believes in Him receives forgiveness of sins." (Acts 10:43)

To this message Cornelius and his household responded.

What is necessary for salvation? To believe in *Him*.

Is it necessary to be convicted of sin, understand why Jesus died on the cross, and then accept His

62

death as a payment for your sins? Of course, there have been millions of people who have followed this path to salvation. I do not doubt their salvation. However, to insist that non-Christians first become convinced of their own sins and then find Jesus at the cross is not the typical pattern we see as people in the Bible became believers.

Consider Peter who had the revelation that Jesus was the Messiah, long before he understood the significance of our Lord's death. Peter confessed to Jesus:

> *"You are the Christ, the Son of the living God."* (Matt. 16:15b)

Our Lord answered Peter saying,

> *"...flesh and blood did not reveal this to you, but My Father who is in heaven."* (Matt. 16:17)

Peter believed.

Consider the blind man whom Jesus healed (John 9). The blind man confessed his faith in Jesus and worshipped Him (John 9:38). Was he saved? Though he did not know the significance of our Lord's death, nor did he even know that Jesus would be crucified, the blind man believed in Jesus. The Bible is clear:

> *"...everyone who believes in Him receives forgiveness of sins."* (Acts 10:43)

63

Consider Zaccheus, the tax-gatherer who welcomed Jesus into his home (Luke 19:1-10). Zaccheus was so impacted by Jesus Christ that he announced his intentions to give half of his possessions to the poor and pay back anyone he had defrauded of anything, four times as much. Seeing this change in heart, Jesus said:

> *"Today, salvation has come to this house,*
> *because he, too, is a son of Abraham."*
>   (Luke 19:9b)

Zaccheus did not understand the death of Jesus, yet, he believed in Jesus.

Finally, consider Paul who was converted while traveling from one city to another persecuting Christians. A light flashed about him and Jesus spoke to Paul from heaven (Acts 9:3-5). Paul became a believer and began to proclaim Jesus in the synagogues, saying, "He is the Son of God" (Acts 9:20). At some point Paul became conscious of his own sinfulness, but first he met Jesus and believed in Him.

This can happen in people's lives today, too. They do not need to follow the Reformed formula of first being convicted of their sins and then applying the answer, which is the death of Jesus. Some people may become Christians simply because God has revealed to them that Jesus is Lord. Of course, God will begin a work in their lives turning them away from sins. The Holy Spirit will convict them of their sins, and begin a process of sanctification, however, consciousness of sins need not precede a person's salvation.

Let me explain this by comparing our relationship to God with children's relationship to their parents. Their relationship, first of all, should be based upon love, acceptance, time, commitment, and all of the other elements that go into a healthy child-parent relationship. When the children grow up, some day they may realize how much their parents sacrificed for their welfare. That realization probably will deepen their own commitment to their parents and cause them to be grateful. However, the child-parent relationship is not dependent upon the child knowing how much the parents have sacrificed. The relationship, first and foremost, is based on love.

Consider the most well-known verse in the Bible.

"For God so loved the world, that He gave His only begotten Son, that whoever believes in Him will not perish, but have eternal life." (John 3:16)

According to this verse, salvation is conditional upon a belief in Jesus Christ. Many Christians equate this with a belief in the fact that Jesus died for our sins. That is the error I am trying to correct here. We are not required to understand the crucifixion. We must believe in the Person—Jesus Christ.

Of course, I wish every human being understood how Jesus died for the forgiveness of our sins. Please do not think I am negating the importance of our Lord's death. However, an understanding of His death—and even a belief in His death—is not what is required for salvation. What actually is required is a belief in Jesus, and the result, which is a vital relationship with God the Father.

This issue becomes especially important when we evangelize Muslims. Most of them already believe that Jesus is a great teacher and prophet. They even believe that He died on a cross. However, they are not Christians. Through study and my own work with Muslims I have come to understand that the most crucial issue for them is in accepting Jesus Christ as the Son of God. Typically, that is the revelation which brings them into the salvation experience.

Similarly, there are other people who may become believers in Jesus without going through the Reformed formula of becoming conscious of sin and then embracing the death of Jesus. Some, such as the blind man, may experience a miracle, and hence, believe that Jesus is the Son of God. Others, as Peter and Paul, may have an encounter with Jesus and, hence, believe in Him

It is not necessary for people to become conscious of their sins or their need for a Savior before they can be saved. Of course, everyone needs the Savior, but God does not require them to have that understanding before they become Christians. They need to believe in the Person Jesus Christ and confess Him as Lord.

Chapter 16
Where the Christian Meets Jesus

When a preacher trained in Death-centered Christianity reminds people of their sinfulness and then offers the cross as the solution, it is not only unbelievers who are expected to respond. Even Christians—who already have placed their faith in Jesus—are reminded of their sinfulness and led to the cross of Jesus. When the people walk out the doors of the church, they are conscious of their sinfulness and grateful to God for His mercy. This impression is imprinted upon their minds, and it can be carried with them for the whole week. Hence, they live their daily lives under the cross—always aware of their sinfulness and always grateful to the Source of forgiveness.

Of course, humility and gratefulness are wonderful attributes in the life of any person. However, is it necessary to induce these qualities by impacting the minds of church-goers again and again with the suffering and death of Jesus?

What if the preacher presents Jesus as risen King and Lord? What if people bow to the Master of the Universe Who has conquered sin and death? What if Christians become overwhelmed by the victorious and loving nature of our God? Humility and thanksgiving also can be induced in the hearts of people who are kneeling at the foot of His throne.

In addition, there is grace at the throne—the type of grace which provides life, power, help, and love. To bow to King Jesus who sits on a throne is an honor. People who yield to the Victorious One rejoice and take strength. They want to shout! Sing! Do good and courageous acts! They willingly go forth in the strength of their King.

In contrast, people who bow to Jesus on the cross must shrink to the lowest of lows. Since Jesus brought Himself to the lowest position in His death on the cross, one who bows there must be lower than a worm, insignificant and unworthy.

When people kneel before God, a dynamic is established in the relationship. Whatever is established in that moment impacts their Christianity throughout their whole lives.

To which position before God should the sincere minister lead his congregation?

Every time the preacher stands in the pulpit, he or she releases a force which either is subduing people or lifting them. A preacher who has been trained in Death-centered Christianity will attempt to bring the listeners to a place of humility, brokenness, and gratefulness at the end of every church service. It is a subdued place. The listener is brought to a meditative state in which he is conscious of his own unworthiness. In that place, there is a stilled submissiveness. A congregational member who has been raised in that environment will not feel as if he or she even has been to church unless he or she is brought to that subdued place in each service.

Of course, everyone needs to hear of our Lord's work on the cross from time to time—humility, submissiveness, and gratefulness are central to the character of one who is Christ-like. However, we are asking fundamental questions about the spirit of our church services. How should Christians feel as they walk out the doors of our churches? Should their heads hang down or be held high? Should they walk in submissiveness or in confidence? What does God want produced in the hearts and minds of people by the time they leave the pews?

Certainly, people need to stop, give God their undivided attention, and worship Him. As King David said, "Surely I have composed and quieted my soul" (Ps. 131:2a). We need that; God expects it. We must seek Him with our whole hearts. Yet, He is alive, in heaven, and pouring out His love upon us. That is primarily where Christians should meet Him. Our destination is not the cross, but God's open arms.

Chapter 17
Crucify Ourselves?

When I hear a Christian say, "We must crucify ourselves," I know I am listening to a person strongly influenced by Death-centered Christianity (or Reformed Theology). Usually they are not aware how profoundly they have been influenced. In fact, their self-degrading statements may sound honorable, humble, and even holy. Yet, in reality, they are based in a misconception of the nature of the Gospel.

To see this, you first must note that nowhere in the Bible are Christians told to "crucify themselves." This terminology has been repeated so many times in some Christian circles that adherents have come to believe that it actually can be found in the Bible. Yet, it is not there.

The apostle Paul does associate crucifixion with the life of the Christian; however, it is always in the context of a finished work. For example, He wrote:

"I have been crucified with Christ...."
(Gal. 2:20)

Notice that Paul considers his crucifixion as something which happened in the past.

The apostle exhorts us to think of ourselves in the same fashion.

Even so consider yourselves to be dead to sin, but alive to God in Christ Jesus.
(Rom. 6:11)

And again,

> *...our old self was crucified with Him,....*
>
> (Rom. 6:6)

Though some Bible translations do not translate accurately the past tense nature of such crucifixion verses, it is consistent throughout the original manuscripts of the New Testament (see also, Gal. 3:3-5; Col. 3:3).

Jesus died on the cross 2,000 years ago. He did that for us. Our job is not to crucify ourselves but to identify with Him and consider our sinful lifestyle as already dead. In practice, that means people who have sinned in the past do not have to review those sins repeatedly and remind themselves how evil they are. The "old self" is dead. It need not be given any attention. Once people have found forgiveness of their sins, they can forget what lies behind and move positively into the future.

There is one verse that encourages us to put "to death the deeds of the body" (Rom. 8:13). However, putting to death "a deed" is very different than putting to death oneself. Of course, there are desires and thoughts in the life of every Christian which are fleshly and should be rejected, denied, subdued, and put to death. However, selectively denying certain fleshly thoughts is very different than killing oneself.

This distinction may be seen more clearly if I explain the phrase "crucify oneself" as it typically is understood by the Christian under Death-centered

Christianity. To crucify oneself or to die entails *meditating on one's unworthiness and subduing one's own desires.*

That is unnecessary.

The reader whose thoughts previously have been molded by Death-centered Christianity may have objections racing through his mind, such as "Death must come before resurrection!" The reader grounded in Death-centered Christianity may fight for his right to die and crucify himself.

Consider carefully the statement that death must precede resurrection. This statement bears some truth, but the death being spoken of by the Reformed thinker is different than the death understood by the Christian with a Life-giving understanding of the Gospel.

In the mind of the Reformed thinker, death entails consciously and repeatedly *seeing oneself as insignificant and then squelching all personal desires.*

In contrast, the healthy Christian realizes that the non-Christian already is living in death— separated from God and without hope in this world (Eph. 2:1-12). Therefore, to step into the resurrection life of Jesus does not require a further death. In fact, there is no place in the Christian life where a person should put themselves to death.

If this is true, why did Paul write in one passage: "I die daily" (I Cor. 15:31)?

If we read the context of these words, we will discover that Paul is *not* talking about seeing himself as insignificant and then squelching all personal desires. The two verses which sandwich Paul's statement, "I

73

die daily," tell about the physical dangers he faced on a daily basis.

> *Why are we also in danger every hour?*
> (I Cor. 15:30)

> *If from human motives I fought with wild beasts at Ephesus, what does it profit me?* (I Cor. 15:32)

A modern missionary living in a very difficult environment, constantly in danger for his life, could join Paul in saying, "I die daily," but these words must not be used by every Christian who thinks he should crucify himself.

Of course, the sincere Christian must take up his cross and follow Jesus (Matt. 10:38). There are certain things that must be sacrificed and certain desires which should be denied in the life of a godly person.

However, it is the *emphasis of Christianity* which we are trying to shift here. The emphasis should not be upon death—but upon life. Healthy Christianity is focused on the Person Jesus Christ Who now sits at the right hand of the Father.

If the correct emphasis is made, then the Christian life is not as difficult as Reformed thinkers would have us believe. Certainly we may carry a burden from time to time as we follow Jesus, but He reassured us:

> *"For My yoke is easy and My burden is light."* (Matt. 11:30)

Think about that—easy—light. The Christian life is not difficult. Following Jesus is a joy. It is a pleasure.

Death-centered Christianity is committed to making life more difficult than it really is. Many truths are seen through a negative lens. They love to sing songs about the old rugged cross and how they must surrender all to Jesus. They often take the words of John the Baptist out of context and say, "Jesus must increase and I must decrease." Of course, their self-degrading statements may have some truth to them. Christians desire to yield to the leading of our Lord Jesus. The cross upon which Jesus died was rugged. But we do not need to imagine ourselves on that cross.

I like to tell Christians they should live their daily lives *on this side of the cross.* This side is the side on which Jesus was resurrected, ascended, and now sits at the right hand of the Father in heaven. He now lives in us and we are alive in Him!

Chapter 18
Christians Have Good Hearts

Christians who want to die or crucify themselves have a fundamental misunderstanding of the Gospel. Not only is the phrase "crucify yourself" not in the Bible, but it is opposed completely to the character of the good news.

To see this you need to realize that before Christians try to die or crucify themselves, they must believe that they are evil. They have accepted the lie (from Reformed theology) that people are evil to the core, and, therefore, self must be put to death.

In reality, part of the good news is that God changes the heart of every believer. Just as clearly as He will remember our sins no more, He also transforms our inner being.

"This is the covenant that I will make
with them
After those days says the Lord;
I will put My laws upon their heart...."
(Heb. 10:16)

God gives every Christian a new heart, and, therefore, every Christian longs within his or her heart to do the will of God.

To help Christians realize this, I like to ask them what they desire for their own communities. Most Christians will answer by saying that they want revival, strong marriages, young people walking with God, prosperity for the community, health, peace, and people loving one another. Notice that these desires are not different than God's desires. The truth is that most Christians want the same things God wants. They have good hearts.

Christians under Death-centered Christianity never can embrace this truth fully. They have emphasized so much the wickedness of humanity that they cannot accept the idea that anyone's heart, even the Christian's heart, may be good.

The Bible verse most often used by Reformed teachers to defend their negative view of the human heart is Jeremiah 17:9, which says:

> *The heart is more deceitful than all else*
> *And desperately sick....*

The King James version says, "desperately wicked." Using this verse, the teacher of Reformed Theology repeatedly impresses upon the minds of listeners how terribly evil every human being's heart is.

In reality, the verse quoted above does not place every person's heart in such a negative light. To see this, all we have to do is read the context of Jeremiah 17:9. The preceding verses—verses five through eight—actually are making a contrast between the life of a person with an evil heart and the life of a person with a good heart.

> *Thus says the Lord,*
> *"Cursed is the man who trusts in*
> *mankind...*
> *For He will be like a bush in the desert...*

Blessed is the man who trusts in the
Lord
And whose trust is the Lord.
For he will be like a tree planted by the
water...."

Do you see the contrast? Some people trust in mankind and others trust in God. Some have evil hearts and some have good hearts. As a result, some are cursed and some are blessed.

Therefore, when we read the next verse which says the heart is deceitful and sick (wicked), we must not conclude that every human being's heart is totally evil. Recognizing this context allows us to look for a different meaning to the phrase, "the heart is deceitful." Jeremiah was focusing primarily on the deceitfulness of the human heart, in the sense that people can rationalize their own sins. For this reason, in the verse following it, God says, "I, the Lord, search the heart..." (Jer. 17:10). Though the heart easily can deceive the person, no one can deceive God.

The main point I am trying to make by looking at this passage is to show how wrong Reformed teachers are to use it and say that every human heart is totally wicked. As Jeremiah wrote, some people do trust in the Lord. Some people are as trees planted by the water. In fact, in the New Testament we can read our Lord's Words concerning Nathanael, that he was a man "in whom there is no deceit!" (John 1:47). Some hearts are not deceitful. Some people do have good hearts.

This point becomes most important when we talk

about the change that happens in a person who becomes a Christian. A central feature of the New Covenant is that God promises to give each one a new heart. If you are a Christian, then you have a new heart. God did not give you an evil heart. Of course, there are passing negative desires, but there also is a deep abiding love and longing to do God's will.

How you perceive your own heart profoundly influences how you live your daily life. Allow me to explain.

Chapter 19
God Works in and through Our Hearts

If your heart is evil, then you cannot trust it. The best you can do during your life is put to death its desires. Deny yourself. Cry out to God, "Not my will be done, but Your will be done!" If you believe your heart is evil, then go ahead and crucify yourself.

On the other hand, if there is anything good in your heart, you can yield to its direction.

Within the New Covenant there are two fundamental promises:

1. Your sins will be remembered no more
2. God writes His laws on your heart

If you are a Christian, then you have a new heart. It is a tablet upon which God is writing His will.

God expounded upon this promise in the Old Testament when He said:

"I will put My Spirit within you and cause you to walk in My statutes, and you will be careful to observe My ordinances." (Ez. 36:27)

Paul explained:

for it is God who is at work in you, both to will and to work for His good pleasure. (Phil. 2:13)

God is not forcing you to do His will, but He is at work in you. The heart of God is joined to your heart. He is breathing within you. He is revealing His will for your life through your own heart.

What does God want you to do in life?

According to Death-centered Christianity you must die to your own desires, that is, determine God's will and then submit your will to His.

According to Life-giving Christianity, a person who has discovered his own true desires has discovered that which God wants him to do. Of course, we all have passing desires which are not in harmony with God's desires, but for the most part, if God wants you to be a businessperson, then you will want to be a businessperson. If God wants you to raise a family, then you will have some desires to raise a family. If God wants you to minister in the church, then you will have desires to minister in the church. God is making His will known to you by causing His desires to rise within your own heart.

Again, this is not to give credence to every passing desire or lust you have. There still will be some desires which are carnal and they must be selectively denied. However, I have good news to tell you about the overall drive, passion, creativity, and vision within your own heart. God likes it. In fact, He is breathing His will into you right there at that entry point of your life.

In light of this truth, consider our Lord's struggle in the Garden of Gethsemane before He gave His life on the cross. Jesus cried out to the Father, "Not My will be done but Thy will be done!" At that moment

Jesus battled with His own desires to subject them to the will of the Father. In like manner, there may be a crucial turning point in your life when you have to subject your own desires. Perhaps you will have a day when you know God wants you to do something, but there are fears and insecurities within you which must be subjected.

However, your everyday life should not be such a battle. Jesus did not live in the Garden of Gethsemane. Neither should you. There may be a life-turning event at some point in your life, but those come rarely. Your day-to-day life should be lived in a relaxed state knowing that God is breathing within your heart and mind, guiding and leading you through your own desires and thoughts.

The distinction I am making here has profound implications on your relationship with God. Think about it. If you must put to death all of your own desires and submit your will to God's will, then you must live as a slave. In fact, that is a good definition of a slave—one who must subject his own will to the will of another.

In contrast, if God wants to help you succeed in life, then He is dealing with you as His child. If you enjoy life and pursue your desires, then you will live as His child. Of course, your Father may correct you from time to time, but His overall heart toward His children is to see them happy and help them succeed in life.

God is not trying to kill you. Just the opposite. He is trying to resurrect you and make you fully alive! If you delight in Him, He will give you the desires of your heart (Ps. 37:4). If you abide in Him, ask whatsoever you desire and it shall be given unto you (John 15:7). God is not out to kill your heart's desires. He is a Father Who wants to help you succeed in fulfilling your desires.

Chapter 20
The Subduing Power of the Cross

Earlier I described Reformed Christianity as the Big Brother of Evangelical Christianity. Big Brother likes to sit in every room where theology is discussed. He faithfully declares to us the finished work accomplished through the death of Jesus. However, Big Brother feels obligated to defend that truth so forcefully that he cannot seem to look beyond the cross and death of Jesus.

If Big Brother reads this book, he may get upset with me. He even may feel that the power of his message is being stolen. For him, the cross has been his focus, his point of impact, and at times, his instrument to subdue listeners. If my Reformed brother cannot bring the people to a place of submission under the cross, how can he produce change?

Let me assure you that I am not taking any power away from the preacher. In fact, I remind my Reformed brothers and sisters that the *good news* is the power of God for salvation (Rom. 1:17). I dare say that there is more power in this message than the message of sin-and-death.

This may be difficult to grasp for a preacher trained in Reformed thinking. They perceive of the human heart as wicked; people as sinful. Therefore, the goal of the preacher is to bring the heart and life of each person into submission. The ministry of the Reformed church is first to offer salvation and second to subdue sin.

At the foundation of every Reformed minister's mission in life is a sincere-felt sense of responsibility to hold evil in check. Along with the Bible, they may use the cross to accomplish this. Let me explain.

Great subduing power lies in this symbol—a vertical piece of wood, with a cross member positioned horizontally. Billions of people have knelt or bowed their heads as they have passed beneath it. Churches all over the world raise this symbol high above their communities, both as a symbol of hope and as a standard by which all can model their lives. Homes the world over have this symbol hanging in kitchens, bathrooms, and bedrooms. Many sensitive children have thought twice about misbehaving under the authority imposed by a cross silently hanging on the wall.

As the symbol of the cross remains ever present, many sincere Christians remain conscious of their need for the cross. They review in their minds the sins they have committed, and every so often they check to see that their own hearts still are bowing to the One Whom they envision hanging on that cross. They live their daily lives under the subduing power of the cross.

Of course, there are many positive results from the presence of this symbol. The world is a better place. Many evils have been avoided. Yet what concerns me is the emphasis of Christianity. What is the message most prominently projected?

I do not believe that the cross should be used as an instrument of suppression—even suppression of evil. God never intended the cross to be used that way.

I do not mean to imply that a minister should abandon all efforts at reducing sin in the world. Of course, the minister is responsible for the care of souls. He or she must warn people to avoid sin and even assertively may rebuke people living in sin. There is a time to confront sinners. Non-Christians should be warned that a judgment day is coming. Christians should be told that their disobedience grieves the heart of God, and He disciplines those He loves. All people must be made aware that sin produces death. It destroys lives. It hurts.

The repentant sinner even may cry at the altar. There is a time to feel sorrow for sins committed. However, sinners should bow to God, not to the cross. They need to recognize Jesus as Lord. He is worthy of our obedience.

In addition, the sinner who desires to turn from sin needs to be reconciled with a God of love. He or she only can hope to find victory over sin by repositioning under Jesus, Who has conquered sin and death. The sinner will be sanctified not by crucifying himself, but by resurrecting into the love and life of a Living God. Life, not death, is the answer.

Chapter 21
Is It Time to Move the Cross?

Fixed at the front of most Roman Catholic churches is a crucifix, that is a cross with the body of Jesus hanging by nails in His hands and feet. Most Protestant churches have a cross without the body of Jesus. Protestants will explain that Jesus is no longer hanging on the cross but has risen from the dead.

Although Protestants have moved in the right direction by removing the body of Jesus from the cross, most of them, and especially Reformed Christians, have not gone far enough. A cross is a helpful reminder of what our Lord has done, but it should be seen as *one of many* accomplishments He has done for His people.

I propose to you that a church with an accurate understanding of the Gospel will not have a cross fixed at the front and center of its sanctuary. It may have a cross located somewhere in the front, but not as the focal point. Or if it does, the cross will be very symbolic, reminding people of the resurrection rather than the death of Jesus.

This may be disturbing to many readers. That is my intent—to challenge your thought patterns. Of course, there is nothing sinful about putting a cross as the focal point of a sanctuary, and I am not advocating every church remove its cross. I simply believe that a cross at the front declares a message not entirely in accord with the true Gospel.

When we study Church history, we learn that the cross was not even used as a symbol in early Christian art. It was not until Christianity came under the dominating influence of church leaders in Rome that crosses began to be displayed. What stands out in early Christian art is Jesus, His resurrection, ascension, and miracle-working life. If we want our churches today to emphasize what the early Christians emphasized, we would be focusing *not* on the cross but on the *life* of Jesus.

Recently, I walked into a Roman Catholic church in a small town in Africa. The building was of a more contemporary design. As I walked into the sanctuary, I could not help but notice that at the front center was a beautiful painting of Jesus rising from the grave and ascending into heaven. A crucifix also was in the sanctuary but it had been moved off to the side. How different this arrangement was from the old cathedrals scattered across Europe in which a crucifix holds the dominant position at the front of each sanctuary.

I could not help but wonder if the leaders of that Roman Catholic church had made the switch. Did they really know how radical of a break they had made from their tradition? Was the design of their sanctuary actually reflecting their beliefs? Did they understand that Jesus, Who was resurrected, ascended, and is alive today is more central to Christianity than the cross of Jesus?

Again, what I am proposing here may be very disturbing to some Christians. Let me repeat that I am not advocating that every church remove their cross. Change is difficult. Change comes slowly. What we must do is re-focus our Christianity gradually.

When we look at changes which took place in the Church in the past, we see how difficult it has been. Beliefs concerning God are life-and-death issues— even eternal issues. The Protestant Reformation did not take place overnight. Years and years of struggle laid the foundation. People died for their new-found beliefs. Leaders helped the masses think through the related issues and the implications of their changing thoughts. In Europe it took about one hundred years for Protestant Christianity to get established firmly.

One of the physical changes resulting from Protestant Christianity was how the church sanctuaries were set up. During the Middle Ages, churches had an altar located below the cross at the focal point, front and center of each sanctuary. With the development of Protestantism, many Protestant groups came to believe that the preaching of the Bible should be the center of the church service. Hence, a pulpit was placed where the altar had been for hundreds of years. Such a change in structure reflected the change in their beliefs.

Many of us have witnessed similar changes in our own lifetimes. During the 1960s to 1980s thousands of Protestant churches removed organs from their sanctuaries. Worship services gradually changed from the sound of a funeral service to a celebration. Rather than people reading from hymnals and following an organist, they sang out boldly, following leaders with guitars, drums, and the most up-to-date sound equipment.

It is interesting how this change in worship style took place. People watched it come, and, though a few resisted, most accepted the idea that change was necessary. Yet many never could make the change. This became most evident the day the organ was removed from the sanctuary. That was the straw that broke the camel's back. Change had become too radical. Hope of returning to how things used to be was gone.

Similarly, today there is a change going on in the Church. The emphasis is shifting from the death of Jesus onto the life of Jesus. As a traveling minister I have the privilege of speaking in hundreds of churches in many countries. It is amazing to see how churches all over the world have experienced a revolution in their worship. Most newer songs are focused on the living God rather than remembering the death of Jesus. Many contemporary churches no longer hang a cross at the front of their sanctuaries.

I wonder how many Christians are comfortable with the changes that are coming. I wonder how many understand the implications.

It is time to face the truth. I declare to you that the life of Jesus is more central to Christianity than His death. This is not just a matter of displaying proper symbols. It is about our belief system. It is about how we live our daily lives. Whether or not this change is made in the church you attend, it is time to make the change within the sanctuary of your heart.

In Closing

I began this book telling you about Sam and his yearning to live right before God. Sam had cried at the altar so many times that he was afraid to do it again, lest he face disillusionment with his own faith. As long as Sam continues to cry at the foot of the cross, he will remain in the clutches of sin and death. He may experience God's forgiveness, but never God's power over sin. Trying to surrender all and putting to death that last bit of personal desire will keep Sam ever-conscious of his own weaknesses and sinfulness.

The answer for Sam is a different lifestyle.

Sam needs to repent toward the Kingdom of God. He needs to posture himself under the Lord who loves him and pours out His grace. Sam needs to develop a lifestyle of bathing in God's love.

In that place there is no condemnation. Sam will no longer review his sins and weaknesses. He will be so overwhelmed with the love of God that shame and consciousness of his own frailties will dissolve.

Walking with the Father, Sam can learn what it means to live as a child. The Father will guide Sam to walk out his own heart's desires. Though he still will have to go through struggles and many learning experiences, Sam will begin to pursue his life-dreams. He no longer will live as a slave of God, but step into freedom as a son. Sam will discover freedom and power through Jesus Christ when he learns to live in the light of His life rather than the shadow of His death.

Appendix

In order to communicate what actually happened at the death of Jesus, let me say that *Jesus took on our sins, but He did not take on the punishment, penalty, or debt for our sins.* There was no punishment nor penalty for our sins, because God the Father forgave our sins. When sins are forgiven, no one has to pay the debt, because the debt has been erased.

It is biblically correct to say that God ransomed us with the life of His Son. We were purchased at a high price. It did cost the Father the life of His Son to win us back to Himself. However, He saved us from sin and death. He purchased us from the world—not paid for our sins.

Concerning the death of Jesus, we can say with biblical accuracy:

1. We were reconciled to God through the death of Jesus (Rom. 5:10; I Peter 3:18)
2. Through His death, Jesus has become the mediator of a New Covenant (Heb. 9:15; 12:24)

Concerning the blood of Jesus, we can say with biblical accuracy:

1. We have been justified by His blood (Rom. 5:9)
2. We have been brought near to God and His promises by the blood of Christ (Eph. 2:13)

3. We have been redeemed with His blood
(I Peter 1:18-19)
4. Through His blood Jesus obtained our
eternal redemption (Heb. 9:12)

Concerning our sins we can say with biblical accuracy:

1. Jesus takes away our sins (John 1:29)
2. He took on our sins (Is.53:5; II Cor. 5:21;
I Peter 2:24)
3. His blood washes away our sins (I John 1:7)
4. Jesus gave His life to put away sin
(Heb. 9:26)
5. God removes our sins from us (Ps. 103:12)

Jesus dealt with our sins, however, there is no verse in the Bible which states nor implies that God the Father inflicted upon Jesus any punishment or penalty for our sins. One phrase that sometimes is used to teach this error is from the book of Isaiah:

*...The chastening for our well-being fell
upon Him....*   (Is. 53:5)

In some Bible translations, the word *punishment* is substituted for *chastening,* hence, the reader may conclude that our punishment or penalty fell upon Jesus.

If we read the whole verse we can see that the chastening or punishment Jesus received was not inflicted by the Father.

But He was pierced through for our
transgressions,
He was crushed for our iniquities,
The chastening for our well-being fell
upon Him,
And by His scourging we are healed.

(Is. 53:5)

The piercing, the crushing, the chastening, and the scourging were inflicted by Roman soldiers. God allowed Jesus to go through that suffering, but that suffering was not the result of God imposing a penalty or taking out His wrath upon the Son.

Concerning the wrath of God, we know that a judgment day will come at some point in the future when God will pour out His wrath upon the world. We can say with biblical accuracy that Jesus will rescue Christians from the wrath to come (I Thes. 1:10; Rom. 5:9). God's wrath remains upon those who will not obey Him (John 3:35), but for those who believe in the Son, God's wrath has been replaced by mercy and grace.

THE COMPLETE WINESKIN (Fourth edition)

The Body of Christ is in a reformation. God is pouring out the Holy Spirit and our wineskins must be changed to handle the new wine. Will the Church come together in unity? Where do small group meetings fit? How does the anointing of God work and what is your role? What is the 5-fold ministry? How are apostles, prophets, evangelists, pastors and teachers going to rise up and work together? This book puts into words what you have been sensing in your spirit. (Eberle's best seller, translated into many languages, distributed worldwide.)

TWO BECOME ONE (Second edition)

Releasing God's Power for Romance, Sexual Freedom and Blessings in Marriage

Kindle afresh the "buzz of love." Find out how to make God's law of binding forces work for you instead of against you. The keys to a thrilling, passionate, and fulfilling marriage can be yours if you want them. This book is of great benefit to pastors, counselors, young singles, divorcees and especially married people. Couples are encouraged to read it together.

GOD'S LEADERS FOR TOMORROW'S WORLD

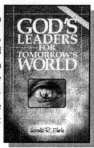

(Revised/expanded edition) You sense a call to leadership in your life, but questions persist: "Does God want me to rise up? Is this pride? Do I truly know where to lead? How can I influence people?" Through a new understanding of leadership dynamics, learn how to develop godly charisma. Confusion will melt into order when you see the God-ordained lines of authority. Fear of leadership will change to confidence as you learn to handle power struggles. Move into your "metron," that is, your God-given authority. You can be all God created you to be!

BRINGING THE FUTURE INTO FOCUS

An Introduction to the Progressive Christian Worldview

What does the future hold? Will there be peace or war? Are the people of God going to rise up in glory and unity or will they be overcome by apathy and deception? Is Jesus coming for a spotless Bride or is He going to rescue a tattered band of zealots out of a wicked chaotic mess? Where is God taking humanity in the Twenty-First Century?

This book will answer your questions and fill you with hope.

Other Books by Harold R. Eberle

PRECIOUS IN HIS SIGHT *A Fresh Look at the Nature of Man*
During the Fourth Century Augustine taught about the nature of man using as his key Scripture a verse in the book of Romans which had been mistranslated. Since that time the Church has embraced a false concept of humanity which has negatively influenced every area of Christianity. It is time for Christians to come out of darkness! This book, considered by many to be Harold Eberle's greatest work, has implications upon our understanding of sin, salvation, Who God is, evangelism, the world around us and how we can live the daily, victorious lifestyle.

YOU SHALL RECEIVE POWER

God's Spirit will fill you in measures beyond what you are experiencing presently. This is not just about Pentecostal or Charismatic blessings. There is something greater. It is for all Christians, and it will build a bridge between those Christians who speak in tongues and those who do not. It is time for the whole Church to take a fresh look at the work of the Holy Spirit in our individual lives. This book will help you. It will challenge you, broaden your perspective, set you rejoicing, fill you with hope, and leave you longing for more of God.

RELEASING KINGS
INTO THE MARKETPLACE FOR MINISTRY

Co-authored by John Garfield and Harold R. Eberle.
This books explains how marketplace ministry will operate in concert with local churches and pastors. It provides a Scriptural basis for the expansion of the Kingdom of God into all areas of society. It paints a picture of Kings who are naturally competitive, creative, and decisive, who are being used to fulfill the Great Commission.

DEVELOPING A PROSPEROUS SOUL
VOL I: HOW TO OVERCOME A POVERTY MIND-SET
VOL II: HOW TO MOVE INTO GOD'S FINANCIAL BLESSINGS

There are fundamental changes you can make in the way you think which will help release God's blessings. This is a balanced look at the promises of God with practical steps you can take to move into financial freedom. It is time for Christians to recapture the financial arena. These two volumes will inspire and create faith in you to fulfill God's purposes for your life.

Other Books by Harold R. Eberle

If God is Good,
Why is there so much Suffering and Pain?

Life isn't fair! Terrorist bombings. Ethnic cleansing. Body-ravaging diseases. Murder. Child abuse. Natural disasters. Genetic maladies. These travesties, global and seemingly relentless, drive us to the limits of our reasoning. When pain and suffering invade our well-laid plans for a good life, we ask the gut question: Why, God, why? In this book, Harold R. Eberle evaluates the role God plays in the Earth, explores the origin of suffering, and reassures us of God kind intentions toward us.

Grace...The Power to Reign

The Light Shining from Romans 5-8

We struggle against sin and yearn for God's highest. Yet, on a bad day it is as as if we are fighting with gravity. Questions go unanswered:

- Where is the power to overcome temptations and trials?
- Is God really willing to breathe into us so that these dry bones can live and we may stand strong?

For anyone who ever has clenched his fist in the struggle to live godly, here are the answers.

The Spiritual, Mystical, and Supernatural

The first five volumes of Harold R. Eberle's series of books entitled, *Spiritual Realities*, have been condensed into this one volume, 372 pages in length. Topics are addressed such as how the spiritual and natural worlds are related, angelic and demonic manifestations, signs and wonders, miracles and healings, the anointing, good versus evil spiritual practices, how people are created by God to access the spiritual realm, how the spirits of people interact, how people sense things in the spirit realm, and much more.

Individual volumes of the *Spiritual Realities* series are available also.

To place an order or to check current prices call:
1-800-308-5837 within the USA or:
509-248-5837 from outside the USA

Worldcast Publishing
P.O. Box 10653
Yakima, WA 98909-1653

E-mail: office@worldcastpublishing.com
Web Site: www.worldcastpublishing.com